interchange

FIFTH EDITION

intro B

Workbook

Jack C. Richards

CAMBRIDGE
UNIVERSITY PRESS

Shaftesbury Road, Cambridge CB2 8EA, United Kingdom

One Liberty Plaza, 20th Floor, New York, NY 10006, USA

477 Williamstown Road, Port Melbourne, VIC 3207, Australia

314–321, 3rd Floor, Plot 3, Splendor Forum, Jasola District Centre, New Delhi – 110025, India

103 Penang Road, #05-06/07, Visioncrest Commercial, Singapore 238467

Cambridge University Press & Assessment is a department of the University of Cambridge.

We share the University's mission to contribute to society through the pursuit of education, learning and research at the highest international levels of excellence.

www.cambridge.org
Information on this title: www.cambridge.org/9781316622407

First published 1994
Second edition 2000
Third edition 2005
Fourth edition 2013
Fifth edition 2017
Fifth edition update published 2021

20 19 18 17 16 15 14 13 12 11 10 9 8 7

Printed in Poland by Opolgraf

A catalogue record for this publication is available from the British Library

ISBN 978-1-009-04041-9 Intro Student's Book with eBook
ISBN 978-1-009-04042-6 Intro Student's Book A with eBook
ISBN 978-1-009-04043-3 Intro Student's Book B with eBook
ISBN 978-1-009-04055-6 Intro Student's Book with Digital Pack
ISBN 978-1-009-04056-3 Intro Student's Book A with Digital Pack
ISBN 978-1-009-04057-0 Intro Student's Book B with Digital Pack
ISBN 978-1-316-62237-7 Intro Workbook
ISBN 978-1-316-62239-1 Intro Workbook A
ISBN 978-1-316-62240-7 Intro Workbook B
ISBN 978-1-108-40605-5 Intro Teacher's Edition
ISBN 978-1-316-62221-6 Intro Class Audio
ISBN 978-1-009-04058-7 Intro Full Contact with Digital Pack
ISBN 978-1-009-04059-4 Intro Full Contact A with Digital Pack
ISBN 978-1-009-04062-4 Intro Full Contact B with Digital Pack
ISBN 978-1-108-40304-7 Presentation Plus Intro

Additional resources for this publication at cambridgeone.org

Contents

Credits

The authors and publishers acknowledge the following sources of copyright material and are grateful for the permissions granted. While every effort has been made, it has not always been possible to identify the sources of all the material used, or to trace all copyright holders. If any omissions are brought to our notice, we will be happy to include the appropriate acknowledgements on reprinting and in the next update to the digital edition, as applicable.

Key: B = Below, BC = Below Centre, BL = Below Left, BR = Below Right, C = Centre, CL = Centre Left, CR = Centre Right, Ex = Exercise, L = Left, R = Right, T = Top, TC = Top Centre, TL = Top Left, TR = Top Right.

Illustrations

337 Jon (KJA Artists): 11, 21, 81; **417 Neal** (KJA Artists): 1, 58; **Mark Duffin**: 7, 12, 26, 37, 41, 52, 70; **Thomas Girard** (Good Illustration): 10, 63, 68, 84; **John Goodwin** (Eye Candy Illustration): 23, 71; **Dusan Lakicevic** (Beehive Illustration): 57; **Quino Marin** (The Organisation): 19, 69, 92, 94; **Gavin Reece** (New Division): 5, 39; **Gary Venn** (Lemonade Illustration): 25, 74, 77; **Paul Williams** (Sylvie Poggio Artists): 6, 29, 67.

Photos

Back cover (woman with whiteboard): Jenny Acheson/Stockbyte/GettyImages; Back cover (whiteboard): Nemida/GettyImages; Back cover (man using phone): Betsie Van Der Meer/Taxi/GettyImages; Back cover (woman smiling): PeopleImages.com/ DigitalVision/GettyImages; Back cover (name tag): Tetra Images/GettyImages; Back cover (handshake): David Lees/Taxi/GettyImages; p. 2 (TL): Yellow Dog Productions/ Iconica/GettyImages; p. 2 (CR): Morsa Images/DigitalVision/GettyImages; p. 2 (BL): Johnny Greig/iStock/Getty Images Plus/GettyImages; p. 3: Nicolas McComber/E+/ GettyImages; p. 4: MichaelDeLeon/iStock/Getty Images Plus/GettyImages; p. 5: Steve Debenport/E+/GettyImages; p. 8 (TL): hudiemm/E+/GettyImages; p. 8 (TC): Marek Mnich/E+/GettyImages; p. 8 (TR): Dorling Kindersley/Dorling Kindersley/ GettyImages; p. 8 (CL): Tpopova/iStock/Getty Images Plus/GettyImages; p. 8 (C): Tpopova/iStock/Getty Images Plus/GettyImages; p. 8 (CR): Creative Crop/ DigitalVision/GettyImages; p. 8 (BR): Betsie Van Der Meer/Taxi/GettyImages; p. 9 (TR): michaeljung/iStock/Getty Images Plus/GettyImages; p. 9 (B): Milk & Honey Creative/Stockbyte/GettyImages; p. 13: Martin Barraud/OJO Images/GettyImages; p. 14 (TL): Lumina Images/Blend Images/GettyImages; p. 14 (TR): Elyse Lewin/ Photographer's Choice/GettyImages; p. 14 (BL): Fabrice LEROUGE/ONOKY/ GettyImages; p. 14 (BR): Susan Chiang/iStock/Getty Images Plus/GettyImages; p. 15 (TL): franckreporter/E+/GettyImages; p. 15 (TR): AWL Images/AWL Images/ GettyImages; p. 15 (CL): Image Source/Image Source/GettyImages; p. 15 (CR): Matthias Tunger/Photolibrary/GettyImages; p. 15 (BL): MATTES RenÃ©/hemis.fr/ hemis.fr/GettyImages; p. 15 (BR): Luis Davilla/Photolibrary/GettyImages; p. 16: Bruce Glikas/FilmMagic/GettyImages; p. 17 (TL): Digital Vision/Digital Vision/GettyImages; p. 17 (CL): Thomas Barwick/Iconica/GettyImages; p. 17 (C): skynesher/E+/ GettyImages; p. 17 (BC): Hans Neleman/The Image Bank/GettyImages; p. 17 (BL): RunPhoto/Photodisc/GettyImages; p. 17 (CR): Portra Images/Taxi/GettyImages; p. 17 (BR): Terry Vine/Blend Images/GettyImages; p. 18: Jupiterimages/Stockbyte/ GettyImages; p. 20: Hero Images/Hero Images/GettyImages; p. 22 (TL): Gabriela Tulian/Moment/GettyImages; p. 22 (TR): James A. Guilliam/Photolibrary/ GettyImages; p. 22 (CL): Stuart Stevenson photography/Moment/GettyImages; p. 22 (CR): Cultura RM Exclusive/Stephen Lux/Cultura Exclusive/GettyImages; p. 22 (BL): Robert Daly/Caiaimage/GettyImages; p. 22 (BR): noelbesuzzi/RooM/GettyImages; p. 24 (TL): Tim Robberts/Taxi/GettyImages; p. 24 (TR): Jan Scherders/Blend Images/ GettyImages; p. 24 (BL): Chris Whitehead/Cultura/GettyImages; p. 24 (BR): A J James/Photodisc/GettyImages; p. 26: Paul Bradbury/Caiaimage/GettyImages; p. 27 (TL): Caiaimage/Trevor Adeline/Caiaimage/GettyImages; p. 27 (TC): Hero Images/ Hero Images/GettyImages; p. 27 (TR): Westend61//GettyImages; p. 27 (CL): Susan Chiang/E+/GettyImages; p. 27 (C): shapecharge/E+/GettyImages; p. 27 (CR): Image Source/Image Source/GettyImages; p. 27 (BL): Henrik Sorensen/Iconica/ GettyImages; p. 27 (BC): Hero Images/Hero Images/GettyImages; p. 27 (BR): Dougal Waters/DigitalVision/GettyImages; p. 28 (Ex 6.1): Hoxton/Tom Merton/Hoxton/ GettyImages; p. 28 (Ex 6.2): Mike Harrington/The Image Bank/GettyImages; p. 28 (Ex 6.3): Alexander Rhind/Stone/GettyImages; p. 28 (Ex 6.4): Vico Collective/Alin Dragulin/Blend Images/GettyImages; p. 28 (Ex 6.5): Leonardo Patrizi/E+/ GettyImages; p. 28 (Ex 6.6): JGI/Tom Grill/Blend Images/GettyImages; p. 28 (Ex 6.7): elenaleonova/iStock/Getty Images Plus/GettyImages; p. 28 (Ex 6.8): Thomas Barwick/ Iconica/GettyImages; p. 30: Tetra Images/Tetra Images/GettyImages; p. 31 (TL): Caiaimage/Sam Edwards/Caiaimage/GettyImages; p. 31 (TR): Shestock/Blend Images/GettyImages; p. 31 (C): Marc Romanelli/Blend Images/GettyImages; p. 32: Dave & Les Jacobs/Blend Images/Getty Images Plus/GettyImages; p. 33: Dan Porges/Photolibrary/GettyImages; p. 33: Sam Edwards/Caiaimage/GettyImages; p. 34: Hero Images/Hero Images/GettyImages; p. 35: Hero Images/Hero Images/ GettyImages; p. 36: XiXinXing/XiXinXing/GettyImages; p. 38: Mint Images - Tim Robbins/Mint Images RF/GettyImages; p. 40 (T): Klaus Tiedge/Blend Images/ GettyImages; p. 40 (B): nwinter/iStock/Getty Images Plus/GettyImages; p. 43 (Ex 1a): Daniel Allan/Photographer's Choice/GettyImages; p. 43 (Ex 1b): Gary John Norman/ Iconica/GettyImages; p. 43 (Ex 1c): Paul Bradbury/Caiaimage/GettyImages; p. 43 (Ex 1d): Dave and Les Jacobs/Lloyd Dobbie/Blend Images/GettyImages; p. 43 (Ex 1e): Hero Images/Hero Images/GettyImages; p. 43 (Ex 1f): BJI/Blue Jean Images/ GettyImages; p. 43 (Ex 1g): XiXinXing/GettyImages; p. 43 (Ex 1h): Phil Boorman/ Cultura/GettyImages; p. 43 (Ex 1i): Gary John Norman/The Image Bank/ GettyImages; p. 43 (Ex 1j): Cultura RM Exclusive/yellowdog/Cultura Exclusive/ GettyImages; p. 44 (Ex 2.1): Portra Images/Taxi/GettyImages; p. 44 (Ex 2.2): Paper Boat Creative/DigitalVision/GettyImages; p. 44 (Ex 2.3): Monty Rakusen/Cultura/ GettyImages; p. 44 (Ex 2.4): Hero Images/Stone/GettyImages; p. 44 (Ex 2.5): diego_ cervo/iStock/Getty Images Plus/GettyImages; p. 44 (Ex 2.6): Caiaimage/Robert Daly/ OJO+/GettyImages; p. 45 (TL): Jetta Productions/Iconica/GettyImages; p. 45 (TR): Dana Neely/Stone/GettyImages; p. 45 (BL): Rob Daly/OJO Images/GettyImages; p. 45 (BR): vgajic/E+/GettyImages; p. 46 (T): Hero Images/Hero Images/GettyImages; p. 46 (B): zoranm/E+/GettyImages; p. 47 (T): HAYKIRDI/iStock/Getty Images Plus/ GettyImages; p. 47 (B): onepony/iStock/Getty Images Plus/GettyImages; p. 48 (Ex 6.1): Klaus Vedfelt/Taxi/GettyImages; p. 48 (Ex 6.2): Caiaimage/Sam Edwards/ Caiaimage/GettyImages; p. 48 (Ex 6.3): Inti St Clair/Blend Images/GettyImages; p. 48 (Ex 6.4): Monty Rakusen/Cultura/GettyImages; p. 48 (Ex 6.5): JGI/Tom Grill/Blend Images/GettyImages; p. 48 (Ex 6.6): Caiaimage/Tom Merton/Caiaimage/ GettyImages; p. 49 (Ex 1.1): Rosemary Calvert/Photographer's Choice/GettyImages; p. 49 (Ex 1.2): Bruno Crescia Photography Inc/First Light/GettyImages; p. 49 (Ex 1.3): Roger Dixon/Dorling Kindersley/GettyImages; p. 49 (Ex 1.4): Alexander Bedrin/ iStock/Getty Images Plus/GettyImages; p. 49 (Ex 1.5): Kaan Ates/iStock/Getty Images Plus/GettyImages; p. 49 (Ex 1.6): David Marsden/Photolibrary/GettyImages; p. 49 (Ex 1.7): RedHelga/E+/GettyImages; p. 49 (Ex 1.8): rimglow/iStock/Getty Images Plus/GettyImages; p. 49 (Ex 1.9): Suwanmanee99/iStock/Getty Images Plus/ GettyImages; p. 49 (Ex 1.10): Creative Crop/DigitalVision/GettyImages; p. 49 (Ex 1.11): Dorling Kindersley/Dorling Kindersley/GettyImages; p. 49 (Ex 1.12): mm88/ iStock/Getty Images Plus/GettyImages; p. 49 (Ex 1.13): kbwills/iStock/Getty Images Plus/GettyImages; p. 49 (Ex 1.14): Steve Wisbauer/Photolibrary/GettyImages; p. 49 (Ex 1.15): Tomas_Mina/iStock/Getty Images Plus/GettyImages; p. 49 (Ex 1.16): Freila/ iStock/Getty Images Plus/GettyImages; p. 49 (Ex 1.17): Paul Poplis/Photolibrary/ GettyImages; p. 49 (Ex 1.18): Dorling Kindersley/Dorling Kindersley/GettyImages; p. 49 (Ex 1.19): Science Photo Library/Science Photo Library/GettyImages; p. 49 (Ex 1.20): Gary Sergraves/Dorling Kindersley/GettyImages; p. 50 (Ex 2.1): Dave King Dorling Kindersley/Dorling Kindersley/GettyImages; p. 50 (Ex 2.2): fcafotodigital/E+/ GettyImages; p. 50 (Ex 2.3): Susan Trigg/E+/GettyImages; p. 50 (Ex 2.4): Davies and Starr/The Image Bank/GettyImages; p. 50 (Ex 2.5): Kai Schwabe/StockFood Creative/ GettyImages; p. 50 (Ex 2.6): Kevin Summers/Photographer's Choice/GettyImages; p. 50 (Ex 3.1): 109508Liane Riss/GettyImages; p. 51 (T): Digital Vision/Photodisc/ GettyImages; p. 51 (B): Lisa Hubbard/Photolibrary/GettyImages; p. 53 (T): MIXA/ GettyImages; p. 53 (B): Tom Grill/The Image Bank/GettyImages; p. 54: Jake Curtis/ Iconica/GettyImages; p. 55 (Ex 1a): Shell_114/iStock/Getty Images Plus/GettyImages; p. 55 (Ex 1b): C Squared Studios/Photodisc/GettyImages; p. 55 (Ex 1c): Image Source/ Image Source/GettyImages; p. 55 (Ex 1d): inxti/iStock/Getty Images Plus/ GettyImages; p. 55 (Ex 1e): skodonnell/E+/GettyImages; p. 55 (Ex 1f): by_nicholas/ E+/GettyImages; p. 55 (Ex 1g): koosen/iStock/Getty Images Plus/GettyImages; p. 55 (Ex 1h): Creativ Studio Heinemann/GettyImages; p. 55 (Ex 1i): Lazi & Mellenthin/ GettyImages; p. 55 (Ex 1j): stockbymh/iStock/Getty Images Plus/GettyImages; p. 56 (T): John P Kelly/The Image Bank/GettyImages; p. 56 (B): Nicola Tree/The Image Bank/GettyImages; p. 59 (T): Zave Smith/Photolibrary/GettyImages; p. 59 (C): XiXinXing/GettyImages; p. 59 (B): Steve Mcsweeny/Moment/GettyImages; p. 60: Dougal Waters/Taxi/GettyImages; p. 61 (spring): Maria Viola/EyeEm/EyeEm/ GettyImages; p. 61 (summer): Dothan Nareswari/EyeEm/EyeEm/GettyImages; p. 61 (fall): Plattform/GettyImages; p. 61 (winter): juliannafunk/iStock/Getty Images Plus/ GettyImages; p. 64 (T): VisitBritain/Britain On View/GettyImages; p. 64 (B): GM Visuals/Blend Images/GettyImages; p. 65 (Ex 6.1): T.T./Taxi/GettyImages; p. 65 (Ex 6.2): Jade/Blend Images/GettyImages; p. 65 (Ex 6.3): Hero Images/Hero Images/ GettyImages; p. 65 (Ex 6.4): Todor Tsvetkov/E+/GettyImages; p. 65 (Ex 6.5): Hero Images/Hero Images/GettyImages; p. 65 (Ex 6.6): Lucia Lambriex/Taxi/GettyImages; p. 65 (Ex 6.7): Er Creatives Services Ltd/Iconica/GettyImages; p. 65 (Ex 6.8): Susan Chiang/E+/GettyImages; p. 65 (Ex 6.9): PhotoAlto/Teo Lannie/PhotoAlto Agency RF Collections/GettyImages; p. 66 (TL): Maximilian Stock Ltd/Photolibrary/GettyImages; p. 66 (TR): Grafner/iStock/Getty Images Plus/GettyImages; p. 66 (CL): Freek Gout/ EyeEm/EyeEm/GettyImages; p. 66 (CR): Vstock LLC/GettyImages; p. 66 (BL): mashabuba/E+/GettyImages; p. 66 (BR): Tom Merton/Caiaimage/GettyImages; p. 70: Nicolas McComber/iStock/Getty Images Plus/GettyImages; p. 73 (bank): Keith Brofsky/Photodisc/GettyImages; p. 73 (coffee shop): Jake Curtis/Iconica/ GettyImages; p. 73 (petrol pump): David Lees/Taxi/GettyImages; p. 73 (book store): Jetta Productions/The Image Bank/GettyImages; p. 73 (clothing store): Blend Images - Erik Isakson/Brand X Pictures/GettyImages; p. 73 (post office): Matt Cardy/Stringer/ Getty Images Europe/GettyImages; p. 73 (supermarket): Johner Images/ GettyImages; p. 73 (pharmacy): Caiaimage/Rafal Rodzoch/Caiaimage/GettyImages; p. 76: Leonardo Patrizi/E+/GettyImages; p. 79 (Ex 1.1): Y.Nakajima/un/ANYONE/ amana images/GettyImages; p. 79 (Ex 1.2): John Lund/Marc Romanelli/Blend Images/GettyImages; p. 79 (Ex 1.3): Maskot/Maskot/GettyImages; p. 79 (Ex 1.4): UniversalImagesGroup/Universal Images Group/GettyImages; p. 79 (Ex 1.5): ullstein bild/ullstein bild/GettyImages; p. 79 (Ex 1.6): Geography Photos/Universal Images Group/GettyImages; p. 79 (Ex 1.7): CommerceandCultureAgency/The Image Bank/ GettyImages; p. 79 (Ex 1.8): Jose Luis Pelaez Inc/Blend Images/GettyImages; p. 80 (Alisha): Dougal Waters/DigitalVision/GettyImages; p. 80 (Kim): Hero Images/Hero Images/GettyImages; p. 82: ullstein bild/ullstein bild/GettyImages; p. 83: Tetra Images - Chris Hackett/Brand X Pictures/GettyImages; p. 85: Westend61/ GettyImages; p. 86 (T): Walter Bibikow/AWL Images/GettyImages; p. 86 (C): Michele Falzone/Photolibrary/GettyImages; p. 86 (B): Takashi Yagihashi/amana images/ GettyImages; p. 87 (Ex 3.1): Photos.com/PHOTOS.com>>/Getty Images Plus/ GettyImages; p. 87 (Ex 3.2): Piero Pomponi/Hulton Archive/GettyImages; p. 87 (Ex 3.3): KMazur/WireImage/GettyImages; p. 87 (Ex 3.4): Nancy R. Schiff/Hulton Archive/ GettyImages; p. 87 (Ex 3.5): API/Gamma-Rapho/GettyImages; p. 87 (Ex 3.6): Jack Mitchell/Archive Photos/GettyImages; p. 88: Christopher Futcher/E+/GettyImages; p. 89: Mel Melcon/Los Angeles Times/GettyImages; p. 90 (T): Kevin Dodge/Blend Images/GettyImages; p. 90 (B): Thomas Barwick/Taxi/GettyImages; p. 91 (L): Stockbyte/Stockbyte/GettyImages; p. 91 (R): nyul/iStock/Getty Images Plus/ GettyImages; p. 93: freemixer/iStock/Getty Images Plus/GettyImages; p. 94: Echo/ Cultura/GettyImages; p. 95: Stockbyte/Stockbyte/GettyImages; p. 96 (T): Thanks for viewing! www.johnsteelephoto.com/Moment/GettyImages; p. 96 (B): Giordano Cipriani/The Image Bank/GettyImages.

I always eat breakfast.

1 Write the names of the foods.

Fruit

1. _____blueberries_____
2. _____
3. _____
4. _____

Vegetables

5. _____
6. _____
7. _____
8. _____

Grains

9. _____
10. _____
11. _____
12. _____

Dairy

13. _____
14. _____

Fats and oils

15. _____
16. _____

Meat and other proteins

17. _____
18. _____
19. _____
20. _____

2 **Complete the sentences with the articles *a* or *an*. If you don't need an article, write Ø.**

1. This is _____*a*_____ tomato.　　**2.** This is _____ yogurt.　　**3.** This is _____ potato.

4. This is _____ egg.　　**5.** This is _____ onion.　　**6.** This is _____ rice.

3 **What foods do you like? What foods don't you like? Write sentences.**

1. fruit

　I like bananas, oranges, and apples. I don't like lemons.

2. drinks

_____

3. vegetables

_____

4. meat and other proteins

_____

5. dairy

_____

6. grains

_____

4 Complete the conversations with *some* or *any*.

1. A: What do you eat for lunch?

B: Well, I usually have ____some____ noodles in broth.

A: That sounds good. Do you have _____ vegetables?

B: No, I don't eat _____ vegetables for lunch.

A: Really? Do you have anything else?

B: Well, I usually have _____ fruit – grapes or strawberries, but I don't eat _____ dessert.

A: Do you drink anything with your lunch?

B: I always have _____ water and coffee. I don't put _____ milk in my coffee, but I like _____ sugar in it.

2. A: What do you want for dinner?

B: Let's make _____ chicken soup.

A: Good idea. Do we have _____ chicken?

B: Yes, we have _____ chicken, but we don't have _____ vegetables. Let's get _____ celery and onions.

A: OK. Do we need _____ pasta for the soup?

B: Yes, let's get _____ pasta. Oh, and _____ garlic, too.

A: Great. We have _____ salt and pepper, so we don't need _____ spices.

B: Yeah, but let's get _____ bread. And _____ crackers, too.

5 What do you need to make these foods? What don't you need? Write sentences.

1. meatloaf

You need some beef, crackers, eggs, and onions. You don't need any oranges.

2. a vegetable salad

_____

_____

_____

3. spaghetti

_____

_____

_____

4. a fish sandwich

_____

_____

_____

5. a fruit salad

_____

_____

_____

6. your favorite food

_____

_____

_____

6 Food habits

A Put the adverbs in the correct places.

1. In Japan, people have fish for breakfast. (sometimes)

<u>In Japan, people sometimes have fish for breakfast.</u>

2. In Canada, people have salad for breakfast. (hardly ever)

_____

3. Some people in South Korea eat pickled vegetables for breakfast. (always)

_____

4. Americans put cream in their coffee. (often)

_____

5. Brazilians make drinks with fruit. (often)

_____

6. In England, people put milk in their tea. (usually)

_____

7. Some people in Mexico eat pasta. (never)

_____

8. In China, people put sugar in their tea. (hardly ever)

_____

B Rewrite the sentences in part A. Use your own information.

1. In Japan, people sometimes have fish for breakfast.

<u>I hardly ever have fish for breakfast. /</u>
<u>I sometimes have cereal for breakfast.</u>

2. _____
_____

3. _____
_____

4. _____
_____

5. _____
_____

6. _____
_____

7. _____
_____

8. _____
_____

7 **How often do you have these things for lunch? Write sentences. Use the adverbs in the box.**

always	hardly ever	never	often	sometimes	usually

1. cheese _I hardly ever have cheese for lunch._
2. pasta _____
3. coffee _____
4. eggs _____
5. beef _____
6. rice _____
7. beans _____
8. salad _____

8 **Answer the questions with your own information.**

1. What's your favorite restaurant?

   _____

2. What do you usually have for dinner?

   _____

3. Do you ever cook?

   _____

4. What's your favorite kind of food?

   _____

5. What's your favorite snack?

   _____

10 What sports do you like?

1 Sports

A Match these sports with the correct pictures.

1. hockey _b_

2. basketball _____

3. bike riding _____

4. swimming _____

5. baseball _____

6. ice-skating _____

7. hiking _____

8. soccer _____

9. tennis _____

10. football _____

B Which sports in part A follow *go*? Which sports follow *play*? Complete the chart.

go		play		
_____ _____		_____hockey_____ _____		_____
_____ _____		_____ _____		_____

2 Complete the conversation. Use the questions in the box.

☐ Does your husband go snowboarding, too?
☑ What do you do on the weekends?
☐ What do you like to do in the summer?
☐ Who do you practice with?
☐ What sports do you like?

Katie: _What do you do on the weekends?_

Isabela: I like to play sports.

Katie: Really? _____

Isabela: Well, I love to go snowboarding.

Katie: _____

Isabela: No, he doesn't like cold weather. He likes to play basketball.

Katie: _____

Isabela: I like to play tennis when the weather is warm.

Katie: _____

Isabela: I practice with my sister. She loves tennis, too.

3 Unscramble the questions. Then answer with your own information.

1. you   do   like   volleyball
   Do you like volleyball?
   Yes, I do. / No, I don't.

2. sports   what   do   watch   you
   _____
   _____

3. you   play   sports   what   do
   _____
   _____

4. swimming   do   you   how   often   go
   _____
   _____

5. do   with   who   sports   you   play
   _____
   _____

4 Write questions and answers about these people.

Maddie

Doug

1. Can Maddie run a marathon?

Yes, she can.

2. _____

_____

Mariana

Felipe and Ken

3. _____

_____

4. _____

_____

George

Ana and Debbie

5. _____

_____

6. _____

_____

5 Write sentences about these people. Use *can*, *can't*, and *but*.

1. He can tell good jokes, but he can't play golf.

2. _____

3. _____

4. _____

6 Choose the correct responses.

1. **A:** Do you like to play soccer?

   B: No, I don't.
   - Yes, I can.
   - No, I don't.

2. **A:** Who do you go bike riding with?

   B: _____
   - I do.
   - My friends from school.

3. **A:** Who can play the piano?

   B: _____
   - Marco can.
   - Yes, he can.

4. **A:** Where do you go hiking?

   B: _____
   - In summer.
   - In the mountains.

7 Can or can't?

A Can you do these things? Check (✓) *can* or *can't*.

	can	can't
1. sing	☐	☐
2. ice-skate	☐	☐
3. build a website	☐	☐
4. drive a car	☐	☐
5. play tennis	☐	☐
6. take good photos	☐	☐
7. speak Japanese	☐	☐
8. swim	☐	☐
9. tell good jokes	☐	☐
10. play baseball	☐	☐

B Write sentences about the things in part A.

1. _I can sing really well._ _____

   _____

2. _I can't ice-skate at all._ _____

   _____

3. _____

   _____

4. _____

   _____

5. _____

   _____

6. _____

   _____

7. _____

   _____

8. _____

   _____

9. _____

   _____

10. _____

   _____

8 Write each sentence a different way. Use the sentences in the box.

☐ He can play sports well. ☐ I love it.
☐ He can't dance at all. ☐ She has many talents.
☑ I hardly ever go hiking. ☐ She tells good jokes.

1. I don't go hiking very often.
   I hardly ever go hiking.

2. He's a great athlete.
   _____

3. She has a lot of abilities.
   _____

4. I really like it.
   _____

5. He's a terrible dancer.
   _____

6. She's very funny.
   _____

9 Answer these questions with short answers. Use your own information.

1. Can you fix a computer? _____
2. Can you speak Spanish? _____
3. Can you act? _____
4. Are you good at sports? _____
5. Are you a good student? _____
6. Do you like your English class? _____
7. Can you play a musical instrument? _____
8. Do you ever go swimming? _____
9. Do you ever play soccer? _____
10. Can you draw very well? _____

10 What can your friends and family do? What can't they do? Write sentences.

1. _____
2. _____
3. _____
4. _____

11 I'm going to have a party.

1 Months and dates

A Put the months in the box in time order.

☐ April	☑ January	☐ May
☐ August	☐ July	☐ November
☐ December	☐ June	☐ October
☐ February	☐ March	☐ September

1. ___January___
2. _____
3. _____
4. _____

5. _____
6. _____
7. _____
8. _____

9. _____
10. _____
11. _____
12. _____

B When are the seasons in your country? Write the months for each season.

Spring	Summer	Fall	Winter
_____	_____	_____	_____
_____	_____	_____	_____
_____	_____	_____	_____

C Write each date a different way.

1. January 11th   ___January eleventh___
2. March 15th   _____
3. November 1st   _____
4. August 16th   _____

5. July 24th   _____
6. May 10th   _____
7. February 2nd   _____
8. December 27th   _____

2 It's January first. How old are these people going to be on their next birthdays? Write sentences.

	Lucas	Liz	Ruth and Sharon	You
Age now	16	32	68	_____
Birthday	April 12th	October 6th	September 21st	_____

1. Lucas is going to be seventeen on April twelfth.

2. _____

3. _____

4. _____

3 Read Tom's calendar. Write sentences about his plans. Use the words in parentheses.

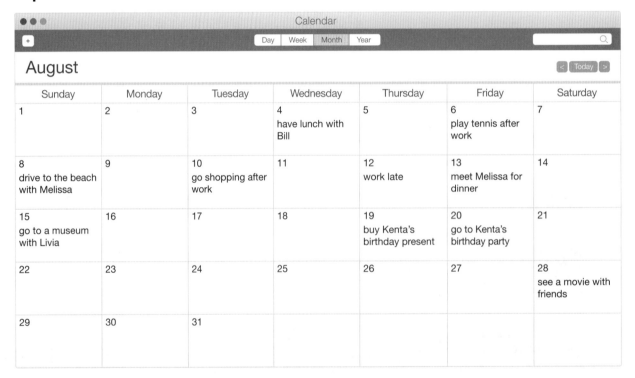

Sunday	Monday	Tuesday	Wednesday	Thursday	Friday	Saturday
1	2	3	4 have lunch with Bill	5	6 play tennis after work	7
8 drive to the beach with Melissa	9	10 go shopping after work	11	12 work late	13 meet Melissa for dinner	14
15 go to a museum with Livia	16	17	18	19 buy Kenta's birthday present	20 go to Kenta's birthday party	21
22	23	24	25	26	27	28 see a movie with friends
29	30	31				

1. On August fourth, he's going to have lunch with Bill. _____ (August 4th)

2. _____ (August 6th)

3. _____ (August 8th)

4. _____ (August 10th)

5. _____ (August 12th)

6. _____ (August 13th)

7. _____ (August 15th)

8. _____ (August 19th)

9. _____ (August 20th)

10. _____ (August 28th)

4 **Complete these sentences. Use the correct form of *be going to* and the verbs in parentheses.**

1. This *is going to be* (be) a very busy weekend.

2. On Friday, my friend Joe and I _____ (see) a movie. After the movie, we _____ (eat) dinner at our favorite Mexican restaurant.

3. On Saturday morning, my parents _____ (visit). They _____ (drive) into the city, and we _____ (go) to the art museum. I think my mother _____ (love) it, but my father _____ (not like) it.
   Later, we _____ (watch) a baseball game on TV.
   My parents _____ (go) home after dinner.

4. On Sunday, I _____ (get up) early. Then I _____ (take) a walk. On Sunday afternoon, I _____ (do) yoga. In the evening, my friend Eve and I _____ (study) together.

5 Complete these conversations. Write questions with *be going to.*

1. **Eric:** <u>What are you going to do this weekend?</u>

   Alex: This weekend? I'm going to go to the city with my son.

   Eric: That's nice. _____ _____

   Alex: We're going to stay at my sister's apartment. She lives there.

   Eric: Really? _____ _____

   Alex: I think we're going to go to a museum.

   Eric: _____ _____

   Alex: No, my sister isn't going to go with us. She's going to go bike riding.

2. **Scott:** I'm going to have a birthday party for Ben next Saturday. Can you come?

   Emily: Sure. _____ _____

   Scott: It's going to be at my house. Do you have the address?

   Emily: Yes, I do. And _____ _____

   Scott: It's going to start at seven o'clock.

   Emily: _____ _____

   Scott: No, Bob isn't going to be there.

   Emily: That's too bad. _____ _____

   Scott: No, I'm not going to bake a cake. I can't bake! I'm going to buy one.

   Emily: OK. Sounds good. See you on Saturday.

6 Next weekend

A What are these people going to do next weekend? Write sentences.

1. _They're going to go_
    bike riding.

2. _____
    _____

3. _____
    _____

4. _____
    _____

5. _____
    _____

6. _____
    _____

7. _____
    _____

8. _____
    _____

9. _____
    _____

B What are you going to do next weekend? How about your family and friends? Write sentences.

1. _____
2. _____
3. _____
4. _____

7 Are you going to do anything special on these holidays or special occasions? Write
sentences. Use the phrases in the box or your own information.

dance	go to a parade	sing songs
eat special food	go to a restaurant	stay home
give gifts	have a party	stay out late
go on a picnic	play games	watch fireworks
go out with friends	play music	wear special clothes

1. Your next birthday

  I'm not going to have a party. I'm going
  to go to a restaurant with my friends, but
  we're not going to stay out late.

2. Your best friend's birthday

_____

_____

_____

3. New Year's Eve

_____

_____

_____

4. New Year's Day

_____

_____

_____

5. Valentine's Day

_____

_____

_____

6. The last day of class

_____

_____

_____

12 How do you feel?

1 **Label the parts of the body. Use the words in the box.**

☐ arm	☐ leg
☐ ear	☐ mouth
☐ elbow	☐ neck
✓ eye	☐ nose
☐ fingers	☐ shoulder
☐ foot	☐ stomach
☐ hair	☐ teeth
☐ hand	☐ toes

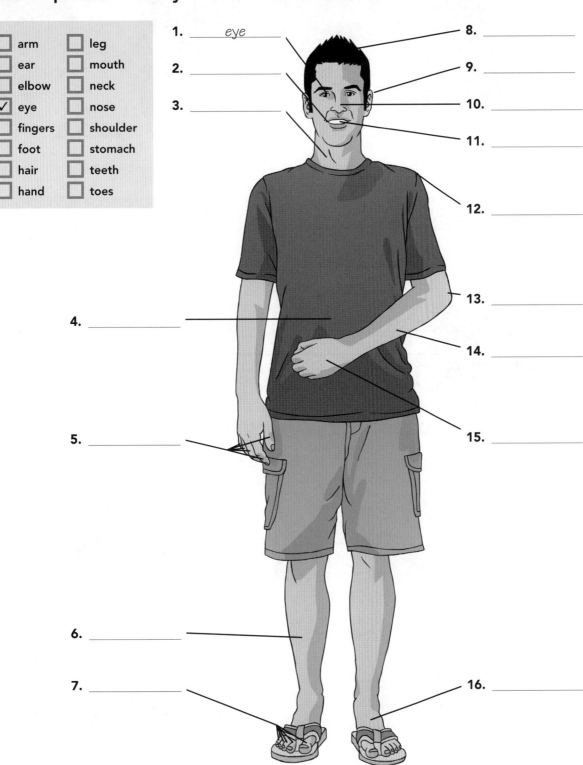

1. _eye_
2. _____
3. _____
4. _____
5. _____
6. _____
7. _____
8. _____
9. _____
10. _____
11. _____
12. _____
13. _____
14. _____
15. _____
16. _____

What's wrong with these people? Write sentences.

1. _He has a toothache._

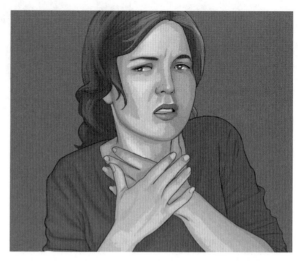

2. _____

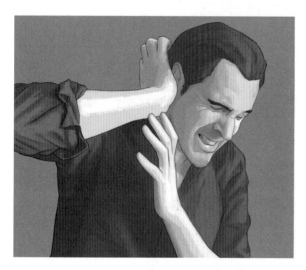

3. _____

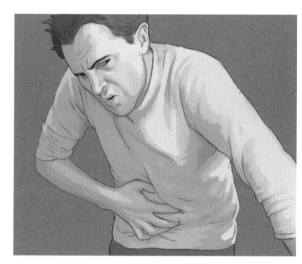

4. _____

5. _____

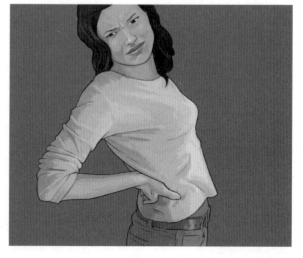

6. _____

3 Complete the conversations. Use the questions and sentences in the box.

Tuesday morning

1. **Jake:** Hi, Camila. How are you?

   Camila: _I'm fine, thanks. How about you?_

   Jake: Not so good. Actually, I feel really awful.

   Camila: _____

   _____

   Jake: I think I have the flu.

   Camila: _____

   _____

   Jake: No, I'm going to go home now.

   Camila: _____

   _____

   Jake: OK. Thanks.

Thursday morning

2. **Camila:** _____

   _____

   Jake: I feel much better.

   Camila: _____

   _____

   Jake: Thanks.

   Camila: _____

   _____

   Jake: Yes, I am.

   Camila: _____

   _____

Tuesday morning

Thursday morning

4 **Complete the sentences with the correct medications.**

1. His nose is very congested. He needs some
   _____nasal spray_____ .

2. I have a horrible cold, so I'm going to buy
   some _____ .

3. Your eyes look red and tired. Get some
   _____ .

4. Alan has a stomachache, so he's going to get
   some _____ .

5. I have a terrible headache. I need some
   _____ .

6. Mandy's cough sounds awful. I'm going to
   give her some _____ .

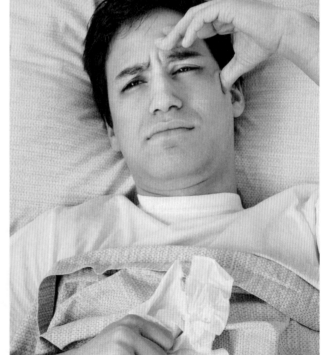

5 **Write each sentence a different way. Use the sentences in the box.**

☐ My head feels terrible.	☑ I'm not happy.
☐ I have a stomachache.	☐ I'm sorry to hear that.
☐ What's wrong?	☐ I'm very tired.
☐ I'm glad to hear that.	☐ I have a sore throat.

1. I feel sad.
   _I'm not happy._____

2. What's the matter?
   _____

3. I'm exhausted.
   _____

4. That's too bad.
   _____

5. That's good.
   _____

6. I have a headache.
   _____

7. My stomach hurts.
   _____

8. My throat is sore.
   _____

6 Give these people advice. Use the phrases in the box.

- [ ] drink some water
- [ ] go home early
- [x] go outside
- [ ] go to the grocery store
- [ ] have a hot drink
- [ ] lift heavy things
- [ ] stay up late
- [ ] work too hard

1. _Don't go outside._

2. _____

3. _____

4. _____

5. _____

6. _____

7. _____

8. _____

7 Write two pieces of advice for each problem.

1. I have a sore throat.   <u>Don't go to work today. Drink some chamomile tea.</u>

2. I have a toothache.   _____

3. I have a cough.   _____

4. I have a cold.   _____

5. I have a stomachache.   _____

6. I have a headache.   _____

7. I have the flu.   _____

8. I have a fever.   _____

8 Health survey

A How healthy and happy are you?
Complete the survey.

How often do you . . . ?

	Often	Sometimes	Hardly ever	Never
get a headache	☐	☐	☐	☐
get an earache	☐	☐	☐	☐
get a cold	☐	☐	☐	☐
get the flu	☐	☐	☐	☐
get a stomachache	☐	☐	☐	☐
stay up late	☐	☐	☐	☐
feel sleepy	☐	☐	☐	☐
get a fever	☐	☐	☐	☐

B Write four sentences about your health. Use the information from the survey in part A.

Examples:

<u>I sometimes stay up late, but I hardly ever feel sleepy.</u>

<u>I hardly ever get a cold or the flu.</u>

1. _____

2. _____

3. _____

4. _____

13 How do I get there?

1 Places

A Complete these sentences with the correct places. Write one letter on each line.

1. I work at a _b_ _o_ _o_ _k_ _s_ _t_ _o_ _r_ _e_ . I love books, so it's a great job.

2. I'm going to go to the ____ ____ ____ ____ . I need a new debit card.

3. My car is almost out of gasoline. Is there a ____ ____ ____ ____ ____ ____ ____ ____ ____ near here?

4. Are you going to the ____ ____ ____ ____   ____ ____ ____ ____ ____ ? I need some stamps.

5. On Sundays, I buy food for my family at the ____ ____ ____ ____ ____ ____ ____ ____ ____ ____ ____ .

6. We're going to have an espresso at the ____ ____ ____ ____ ____ ____ ____ ____ ____ ____ before class.

7. Anita is going to get some medicine at the ____ ____ ____ ____ ____ ____ ____ ____ ____ .

8. My son is going to school next week. We're going to the ____ ____ ____ ____ ____ ____ ____ ____ ____   ____ ____ ____ ____ ____ downtown to buy him a backpack.

B Match the pictures to the places in part A.

2 Look at the map. Complete the sentences with the prepositions in the box.

☐ across from   ☐ between   ✓ on
☐ behind   ☐ next to   ☐ on the corner of

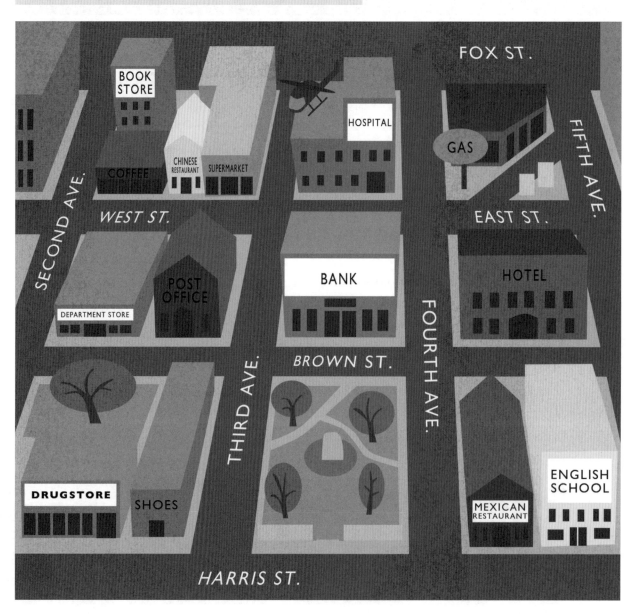

1. The department store is _____on_____ Brown Street.
2. The hospital is _____ the bank.
3. The bookstore is _____ Fox Street and Second Avenue.
4. The Chinese restaurant is on West Street, _____ the coffee shop and the supermarket.
5. The shoe store is _____ the drugstore.
6. The Mexican restaurant is _____ the park.

3 Where is it?

A Look at the map in Exercise 2 again. Where is each place? Write two sentences.

1. post office   <u>The post office is on the corner of Brown Street</u>
<u>and Third Avenue. It's next to the department store.</u>

2. supermarket   _____

_____

3. English school   _____

_____

4. gas station   _____

_____

5. coffee shop   _____

_____

6. hotel   _____

_____

7. drugstore   _____

_____

8. bank   _____

_____

B Where is your school? Draw a map. Then write two sentences.

_____

_____

4 Complete the conversation. Use the sentences and questions in the box.

- ☑ Excuse me. Can you help me?
- ☐ Is there a restroom around here?
- ☐ Next to the Chinese restaurant?
- ☐ Thanks a lot.
- ☐ Where on West Street?

Tom: _Excuse me. Can you help me?_

Woman: Sure.

Tom: _____

Woman: Yes, there is. It's in the supermarket on West Street.

Tom: _____

Woman: It's on the corner of West Street and Third Avenue.

Tom: _____

Woman: Yes, that's right. It's right next to the Chinese restaurant.

Tom: _____

Woman: You're welcome.

5 Complete the sentences with the opposites.

1. The post office isn't on the right. It's on the _____left_____ .
2. The Empire State Building is far from here, but Central Park is _____ here. You can walk there.
3. Don't walk down Columbus Avenue. Walk _____ Columbus Avenue.
4. The New London Hotel isn't in front of the bank. It's _____ it.
5. Don't turn left on Sixteenth Street. Turn _____ .

6 Look at the map. Give these people directions. Use the phrases and sentences in the box.

It's on the left/right.   Walk down/Go down . . . Street/Avenue.
Turn left on . . . Street/Avenue.   Walk to . . . Street/Avenue.
Turn right on . . . Street/Avenue.   Walk up/Go up . . . Street/Avenue.

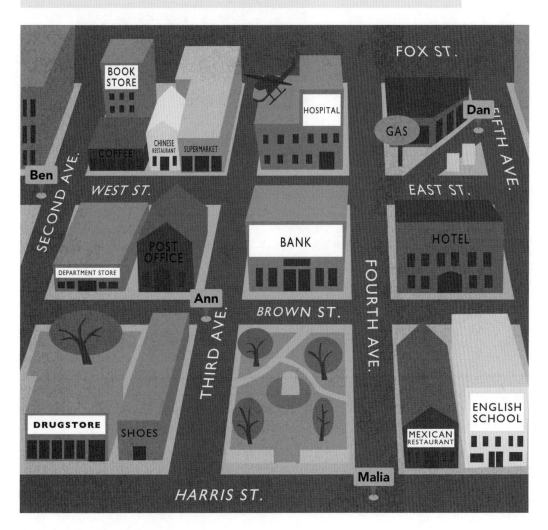

1. Dan is looking for the department store.

   Walk down Fifth Avenue. Turn right on Brown Street.

   Walk to Second Avenue. It's on the right.

2. Malia is looking for the Chinese restaurant.

   _____

   _____

3. Ben is looking for the Mexican restaurant.

   _____

   _____

4. Ann is looking for the bookstore.

   _____

   _____

7 **Imagine you're going to have a party. Complete the invitation. Then draw a map and write directions to the party from your school.**

MAP TO THE PARTY

PARTY

DATE: _____

TIME: _____

PLACE: _____

DIRECTIONS TO THE PARTY

Start at the school. Then _____

_____

_____

_____

14 I had a good time.

1 Last Saturday

A What did these people do last Saturday? Write sentences.

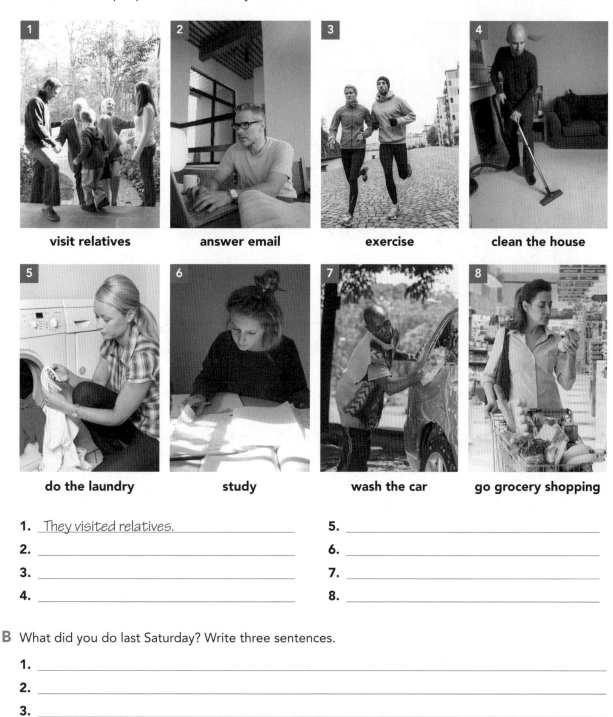

1   **visit relatives** 2   **answer email** 3   **exercise** 4   **clean the house**

5   **do the laundry** 6   **study** 7   **wash the car** 8   **go grocery shopping**

1. _They visited relatives._   5. _____

2. _____   6. _____

3. _____   7. _____

4. _____   8. _____

B What did you do last Saturday? Write three sentences.

1. _____

2. _____

3. _____

2 Kim and Alisha are sending text messages. Complete the sentences. Use the simple past form of the verbs in parentheses.

Messages

Alisha

How was your weekend?

Kim

It was really busy. I ____worked____ (work) on Friday, then I _____ (invite) friends over after work. I _____ (cook) dinner for them. We _____ (listen) to music and _____ (talk) about work, but they _____ (not stay) very late.

Alisha

What did you do on Saturday and Sunday?

Kim

I _____ (get up) early on Saturday because I _____ (play) basketball with Angela. Then I _____ (visit) relatives. We _____ (walk) downtown and _____ (eat) dinner. Oh, and we _____ (see) a movie. On Sunday, I _____ (study) for my math test with my friends. I _____ (do) laundry on Sunday afternoon, too.

Alisha

Wow! That was a busy weekend! I _____ (not do) much this weekend. I _____ (answer) email on Friday night and I _____ (watch) TV, too. On Saturday, I _____ (not get up) early. I _____ (clean) the house and I _____ (go) grocery shopping. I _____ (not do) anything on Sunday!

3 **Claudia and Hiro did different things last weekend. Write sentences about them.**

Claudia

Hiro

1. watch TV   <u>Claudia watched TV. Hiro didn't watch TV.</u>

2. go to a museum   _____

3. ride a bicycle   _____

4. cook   _____

5. study   _____

6. shop   _____

7. play tennis   _____

4 Complete the chart.

Present	Past	Present	Past
buy	_bought_	go	_____
come	_____	_____	had
_____	did	read	_____
eat	_____	ride	_____
_____	felt	_____	saw
_____	met	sit	_____

5 Complete the conversation. Use the simple past forms of the verbs in parentheses.

Aaron: So, Beth, _____did_____ you

_____have_____ (have) a good summer?

Beth: Well, I _____ (have) an interesting

summer. My sister and her family

_____ (come) to visit for two weeks.

Aaron: That's nice.

Beth: Yes and no. My sister _____ (not feel)

well, so she _____ (sit) on the sofa

and _____ (watch) TV. She hardly ever

_____ (get up).

Aaron: Oh, well. _____ her husband and kids

_____ (have) a good time?

Beth: I think so. They _____ (play) volleyball

and _____ (ride) their bikes every day.

Aaron: _____ you _____ (go out) to

any restaurants?

Beth: No, I _____ (cook) breakfast,

lunch, and dinner every day.

They _____ (eat) a lot of food, but

they _____ (not wash) any dishes.

Aaron: That's too bad. _____ you _____ (relax) at all last summer?

Beth: Yes. My sister and her family finally _____ (go) home, and then

I _____ (relax). I just _____ (read) some books and

_____ (listen) to music.

6 **Unscramble the questions about last summer. Then answer with your own information.**

Last summer, . . . ?

1. did   any   books   you   read   good

    A: _Did you read any good books?_

    B: _Yes, I did. I read three great books. / No, I didn't. I read one boring book._

2. go   interesting   anywhere   you   did

    A: _____

    B: _____

3. any   take   did   you   pictures

    A: _____

    B: _____

4. buy   you   did   anything   interesting

    A: _____

    B: _____

5. did   eat   you   foods   any   new

    A: _____

    B: _____

6. games   did   you   any   play

    A: _____

    B: _____

7. you   did   sports   play   any

    A: _____

    B: _____

8. you   did   interesting   meet   any   people

    A: _____

    B: _____

9. any   see   you   did   movies   good

    A: _____

    B: _____

7 Summer activities

A The Johnson family did many fun activities last summer. Write sentences about them.

1. <u>They rode horses.</u>

2. _____

3. _____

4. _____

5. _____

6. _____

7. _____

8. _____

B Write sentences about your activities last summer.

1. _____

2. _____

3. _____

4. _____

1 **Complete the conversation. Use the sentences in the box.**

☐ I was sixteen.	☐ No, it wasn't. I loved it!
☑ No, I wasn't. I was born in Europe.	☐ No, I'm from Belgium.
☐ We came here for my father's job.	☐ We moved here in 2009.
☐ I was born in Brussels.	☐ Yes, they were. We were all born there.

Jason: Were you born here in the U.S., Marie?

Marie: _No, I wasn't. I was born in Europe._

Jason: Oh, were you born in France?

Marie: _____

Jason: Really? What city were you born in?

Marie: _____

Jason: Were your parents born in Brussels, too?

Marie: _____

Jason: And why did you come to the U.S.?

Marie: _____

Jason: So when did you move here?

Marie: _____

Jason: Really? How old were you then?

Marie: _____

Jason: Was it scary?

Marie: _____

2 Complete these conversations with *was*, *wasn't*, *were*, or *weren't*.

1. **Sandra:** _____Were_____ you born in
   the U.S., Ivan?

   Ivan: Yes, I _____ . My brother and I
   _____ born here in Miami.

   Sandra: I _____ born here, too. What
   about your parents? _____
   they born here?

   Ivan: Well, my father _____ . He
   _____ born in Cuba, but my
   mother _____ born in the
   U.S. – in Detroit.

   Sandra: Detroit? Really? My parents
   _____ born in Detroit, too!

2. **Kristin:** I called you on Saturday, but you
   _____ home.

   Jennifer: No, I _____ . I _____
   at the beach all weekend.

   Kristin: That's nice. How _____ the
   weather there?

   Jennifer: It _____ beautiful.

   Kristin: _____ your parents there?

   Jennifer: No, they _____ . I
   _____ with my sister. It
   _____ great!

3. **Mindy:** _____ you in college last
   year, Alan?

   Alan: No, I _____ . I graduated from
   college two years ago.

   Mindy: So where _____ you last year?

   Alan: I _____ in Japan.

   Mindy: Oh! _____ you in Tokyo?

   Alan: No, I _____ . I _____
   in Osaka. I had a job there.

   Mindy: What _____ the job?

   Alan: I _____ an English teacher.

3 Write four sentences about each person.

Marie Curie, scientist (1867–1934)
- born in Poland
- won Nobel Prizes in 1903 and 1911

Gabriel García Márquez, author (1927–2014)
- born in Colombia
- wrote *One Hundred Years of Solitude*, 1967

Maya Angelou, author (1928–2014)
- born in the U.S.
- wrote *I Know Why the Caged Bird Sings*, 1969

Pat Morita, actor (1932–2005)
- born in the U.S.
- was in the movie *The Karate Kid*, 1984

Grace Kelly, actress (1929–1982)
- born in the U.S.
- married Prince Rainier III of Monaco, 1956

Salvador Dalí, artist (1904–1989)
- born in Spain
- painted *The Persistence of Memory*, 1931

1. Marie Curie was a scientist. She was born in 1867 in Poland. She won Nobel Prizes in 1903 and 1911. She died in 1934.

2. _____

3. _____

4. _____

5. _____

6. _____

4 Complete these questions. Use the words in the box.

☐ How ☐ How old ☑ What ☐ When ☐ Where ☐ Who ☐ Why

1. **A:** _____What_____ was your favorite subject in high school?

   B: It was art.

2. **A:** _____ was your favorite teacher?

   B: My art teacher, Mrs. Heintz.

3. **A:** _____ did you graduate from high school?

   B: In 2006.

4. **A:** _____ did you go to college?

   B: I went to Duke University.

5. **A:** _____ did you study physics?

   B: Because I wanted to become an astronaut!

6. **A:** _____ were your professors in college?

   B: They were great.

7. **A:** _____ were you when you graduated?

   B: I was 22 years old.

5 Write whether each sentence is *true* or *false*. Correct the false sentences.

1. Students usually go to middle school before elementary school.

   <u>False. Students usually go to middle school after elementary school. /</u>
   <u>Students usually go to elementary school before middle school.</u>

2. Students often study in the library.

   _____

3. Students never eat lunch in the cafeteria.

   _____

4. Physical education classes are almost always in an auditorium.

   _____

5. Students usually study history and science in high school.

   _____

6 Unscramble the questions about your elementary school days. Then answer with your own information.

1. was your of school how first day

    A: <u>How was your first day of school?</u>

    B: _____

2. your was teacher who favorite

    A: _____

    B: _____

3. favorite was your what class

    A: _____

    B: _____

4. your who best were friends

    A: _____

    B: _____

5. spend did your where you free time

    A: _____

    B: _____

6. leave did when you elementary school

    A: _____

    B: _____

7 Childhood memories

A Complete the questions with *did*, *was*, or *were*. Then answer the questions. Use short answers.

1. **A:** _____Were_____ you born here?
   B: _Yes, I was. / No, I wasn't._

2. **A:** _____ you grow up in a big city?
   B: _____

3. **A:** _____ you play sports?
   B: _____

4. **A:** _____ your home near your school?
   B: _____

5. **A:** _____ you ride a bus to school?
   B: _____

6. **A:** _____ you a good student?
   B: _____

7. **A:** _____ your teachers nice?
   B: _____

8. **A:** _____ you have a lot of friends?
   B: _____

9. **A:** _____ your grandparents live near you?
   B: _____

10. **A:** _____ both your parents work?
    B: _____

B Write sentences about your childhood.

1. _____
   _____

2. _____
   _____

3. _____
   _____

4. _____
   _____

5. _____
   _____

6. _____
   _____

1 **Make a phone conversation. Use the sentences and questions in the box.**

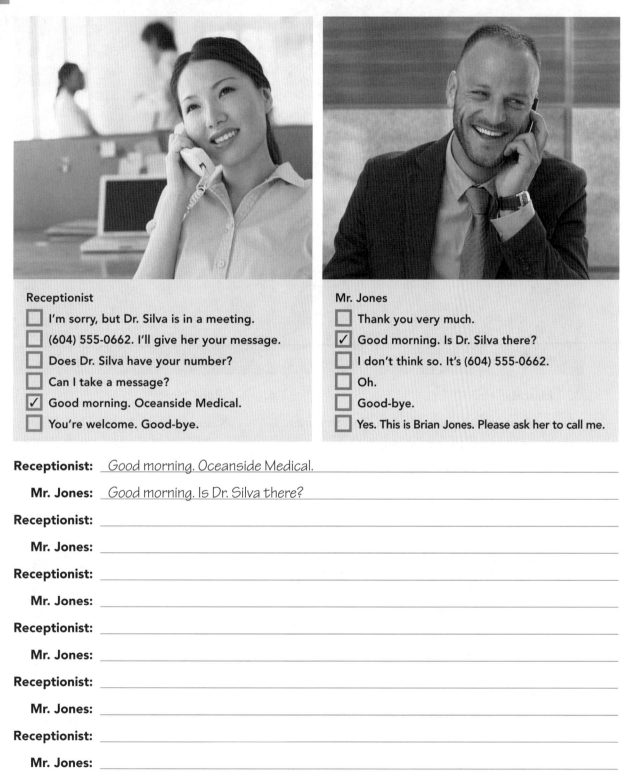

Receptionist

☐ I'm sorry, but Dr. Silva is in a meeting.

☐ (604) 555-0662. I'll give her your message.

☐ Does Dr. Silva have your number?

☐ Can I take a message?

☑ Good morning. Oceanside Medical.

☐ You're welcome. Good-bye.

Mr. Jones

☐ Thank you very much.

☑ Good morning. Is Dr. Silva there?

☐ I don't think so. It's (604) 555-0662.

☐ Oh.

☐ Good-bye.

☐ Yes. This is Brian Jones. Please ask her to call me.

Receptionist: *Good morning. Oceanside Medical.*

Mr. Jones: *Good morning. Is Dr. Silva there?*

Receptionist: _____

Mr. Jones: _____

Receptionist: _____

Mr. Jones: _____

Receptionist: _____

Mr. Jones: _____

Receptionist: _____

Mr. Jones: _____

Receptionist: _____

Mr. Jones: _____

2 **Kate called her friends yesterday. Where were they? Complete the conversations. Use the words in the box.**

☐ bed ☐ hospital ☐ library ☑ mall ☐ vacation ☐ work

1. **Sally:** Hello?

    Kate: Hello, Sally? It's Kate.

    Sally: Oh, hi, Kate. Listen. I can't talk right now. I'm _at the mall_ . Call me later?

2. **Jay:** Hello?

    Kate: Hey, Jay. It's –

    Jay: Kate. Sorry, can you call me in the morning? I'm _____ .

3. **Marcela:** Hello?

    Kate: Hi, Marcela. It's Kate. Do you want to see a movie tonight?

    Marcela: I'd love to, but I can't. I'm _____ with my parents.

4. **Bob:** Hello?

    Kate: Hi, Bob. It's Kate. You know, you sound terrible. Are you OK?

    Bob: Not really. I'm _____ . I broke my leg!

5. **Angie:** Hello?

    Kate: Hello, Angie? It's Kate. Why are you whispering? Where are you?

    Angie: Oh, I'm _____ .

6. **Pedro:** Hello?

    Kate: Hey, Pedro. Do you have a minute?

    Pedro: Not really. I'm _____ . Call me tonight.

3 Unscramble the sentences.

1. with   night   I   him   studied   last   .

I studied with him last night.

2. you   help   I   can   ?

_____

3. her   the   gave   they   book   .

_____

4. remember   you   me   do   ?

_____

5. his   I   call   missed   yesterday   .

_____

6. weekend   last   we   them   visited   .

_____

4 Heidi is checking her voice-mail messages. Complete the messages with the correct pronouns.

Ann's message

Hello, Miss Anderson. This is Ann Lopez. _____I_____
work at First City Bank. _____ left your
wallet here this morning. Please call _____
at (808) 555-1247. I'd like to give it back to
_____ before we close today.

Jim's message

Hey, Heidi. It's Jim. I'm sorry _____
missed your call yesterday. Listen, my friends and I
are going to go out for coffee tomorrow morning.
_____ 're meeting at my house at 9:00.
Would you like to join _____ ? Give
_____ a call!

Sarah's message

Hi, Heidi. It's Sarah. Did you see Marco today?
_____ 's having a birthday party on Friday.
Do you want to go with _____ ? I'm
going to buy _____ a present later. Call
_____ ! Thanks!

5 Complete the phone conversation. Use the words in the box.

☐ at	☐ call	☐ does	☐ her	☐ please
☐ but	☑ can	☐ have	☐ in	☐ this

Allison: Hello?

Evan: Hello. _____Can_____ I speak to Roberta, _____ ?

Allison: I'm sorry, _____ she's _____ a meeting. Can I give _____ a message?

Evan: Yes. _____ is Evan Martin. Please ask her to _____ me. I'm _____ work.

Allison: Does she _____ your number?

Evan: Yes, she _____ .

6 Complete the excuses. Use your own ideas.

1. **A:** Can you drive me to class this evening?
   B: I'm sorry, but I have to _____babysit_____ .

2. **A:** Do you want to see a movie with me this weekend?
   B: I'd like to, but I need to _____ .

3. **A:** Can you walk my dog on Sunday?
   B: I'm sorry, but I can't. I have to _____ .

4. **A:** Can you help me with my homework tonight?
   B: I'm sorry, but I can't. I have to _____ .

5. **A:** Would you like to play tennis on Saturday?
   B: I'd like to, but I need to _____ .

6. **A:** Can you go to the mall this weekend?
   B: I'm sorry, but I have to _____ .

7 Imagine your friends invite you to do these things. Accept or refuse their invitations as indicated. Use the phrases and sentences in the box.

Accepting	Refusing and making excuses
I'd love to.	I'm sorry, but I can't. I have to / need to / want to . . .
I'd like to.	I'd like to, but I have to / need to / want to . . .

1. **A:** Do you want to play soccer with us this afternoon?

   B: (refuse) _I'd like to, but I have to work._

2. **A:** Do you want to have dinner with me tomorrow?

   B: (refuse) _____

   _____

3. **A:** Do you want to study at my house after class?

   B: (accept) _____

4. **A:** Do you want to go swimming with me on Saturday morning?

   B: (accept) _____

5. **A:** Do you want to go hiking with me this weekend?

   B: (refuse) _____

   _____

8 Complete each sentence with *like to*, *love to*, or *want to*.

1. **A:** Would you _____like to_____ go to Bill's party on Thursday night?

   B: I'd _____ go, but I have to study. I have a test on Friday.

2. **A:** Do you _____ play tennis after work?

   B: I'd _____ , but I have to work late.

3. **A:** Would you _____ have dinner at our house?

   B: Yes, I'd _____ !

4. **A:** Do you _____ visit the science museum tomorrow?

   B: I'd _____ go, but I already have plans.

5. **A:** Would you _____ go to the movies tonight?

   B: Yes, but I don't _____ see *Horror House 3*. I don't like scary movies!

6. **A:** Do you _____ leave a message?

   B: Yes, please tell Dr. O'Brien that I'd _____ speak with her about our meeting.

9 Answer the questions. Write sentences with *like to*, *want to*, and *need to*.

1. Where are two places you want to visit?

I want to visit Seoul, South Korea.

I want to visit Rio de Janeiro, Brazil.

2. What are two things you like to do often?

_____

_____

3. What are two things you need to do this week?

_____

_____

4. Who are two famous people you want to meet?

_____

_____

5. What are two foods you like to eat?

_____

_____

6. What are two things you want to do this year?

_____

_____

7. What are two things you like to do after class?

_____

_____

8. Where are two places you like to go on weekends?

_____

_____